I0385232

· TATTOO ·
INSPIRATION
· COMPENDIUM ·
OF ORNAMENTAL DESIGNS FOR TATTOO ARTISTS and DESIGNERS

EDITIONS Vault

INTRODUCTION

Ornamentation has been an integral part of the design process for centuries. In the Middle Ages, ornamentation was a powerful way to visually express prosperity and prestige in an era of limited materials. Intricate carved wooden panels adorned with decorative flourishes made from precious metals were popular among the wealthy. During the Industrial Revolution (1760-1840), manufacturing techniques allowed ornaments to be mass-produced, bringing elegant and beautiful artistic designs to mainstream culture. The ability to create compelling shapes without gold or expensive materials was revolutionary at the time, and cut crystal chandeliers, elaborate furnishings and floral wallpaper became ubiquitous symbols of elegance. Ornamentation has remained relevant in modern design, often informing contemporary trends in furniture design, high-end fashion, and graphic and tattoo design.

This comprehensive guide to ornamentation contains 157 high-resolution downloadable images of beautifully intricate designs, perfect for experienced artists and beginners. With this book, you'll be able to create complex designs quickly and easily, with no guesswork involved. From intricate rococo ornaments to ornate floral designs, there's something for everyone in this compendium.

Disclaimer:
Vault Editions Ltd. believes that the images in this book are no longer protected by copyright and are in the public domain, after taking reasonable steps to determine their copyright status. However, please note that Vault Editions Ltd. cannot guarantee that your use of the images will not infringe the rights of third parties. It is your responsibility to conduct your own analysis and satisfy any copyright or other conditions for your proposed use of the images.

vaulteditions.com

DOWNLOAD YOUR FILES

Downloading your files is simple. To access your digital files, please go to the last page of this book and follow the instructions.

For technical assistance, please email:
info@vaulteditions.com

Copyright
Copyright © Vault Editions Ltd 2023.

Bibliographical Note

This book is a new work created by Vault Editions Ltd.

ISBN: 978-1-922966-06-3

TATTOO INSPIRATION COMPENDIUM

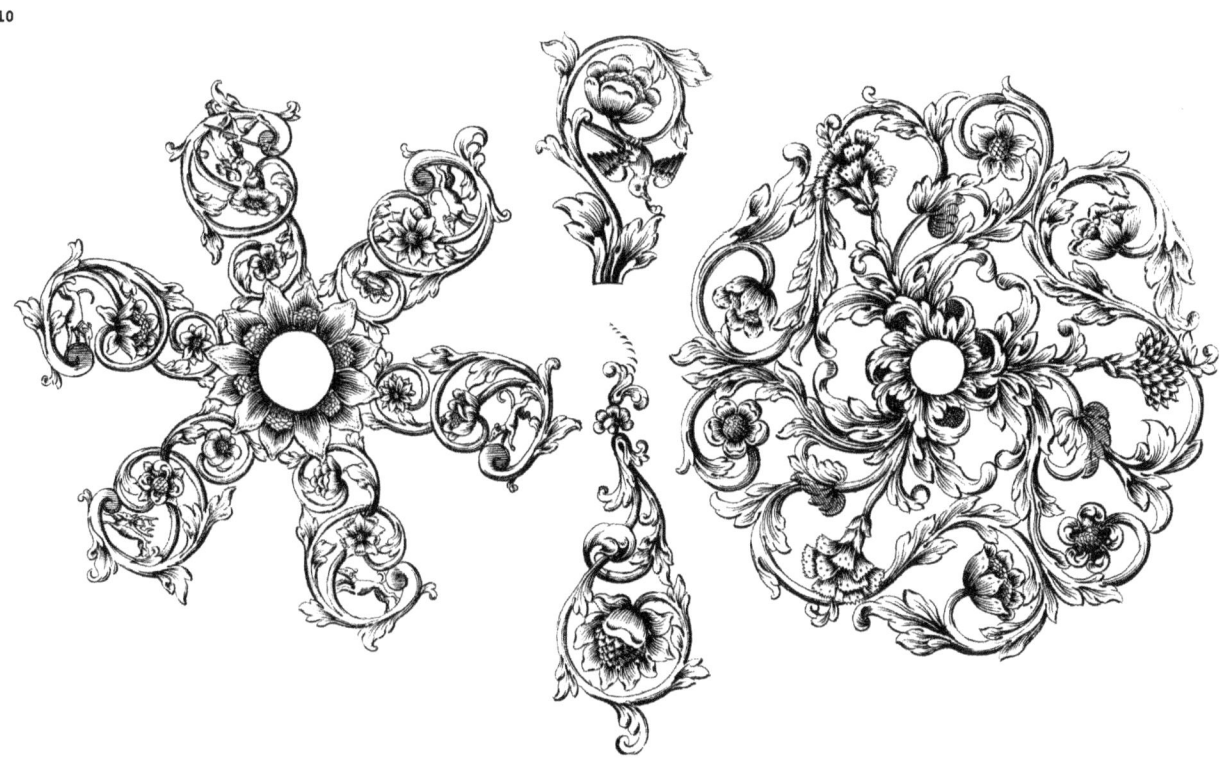

15

16

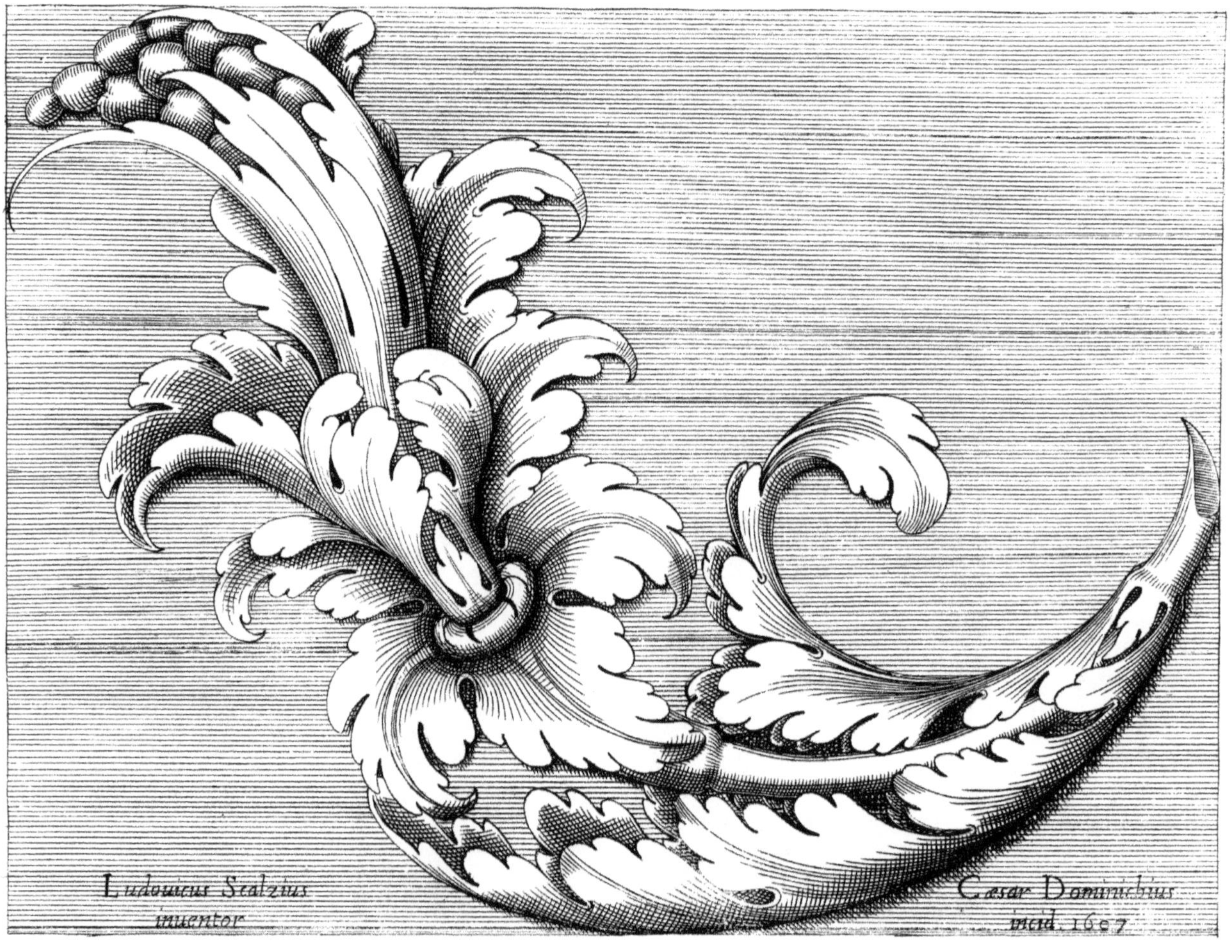
Ludouicus Scalzius
inuentor
Cæsar Dominichius
incid. 1607

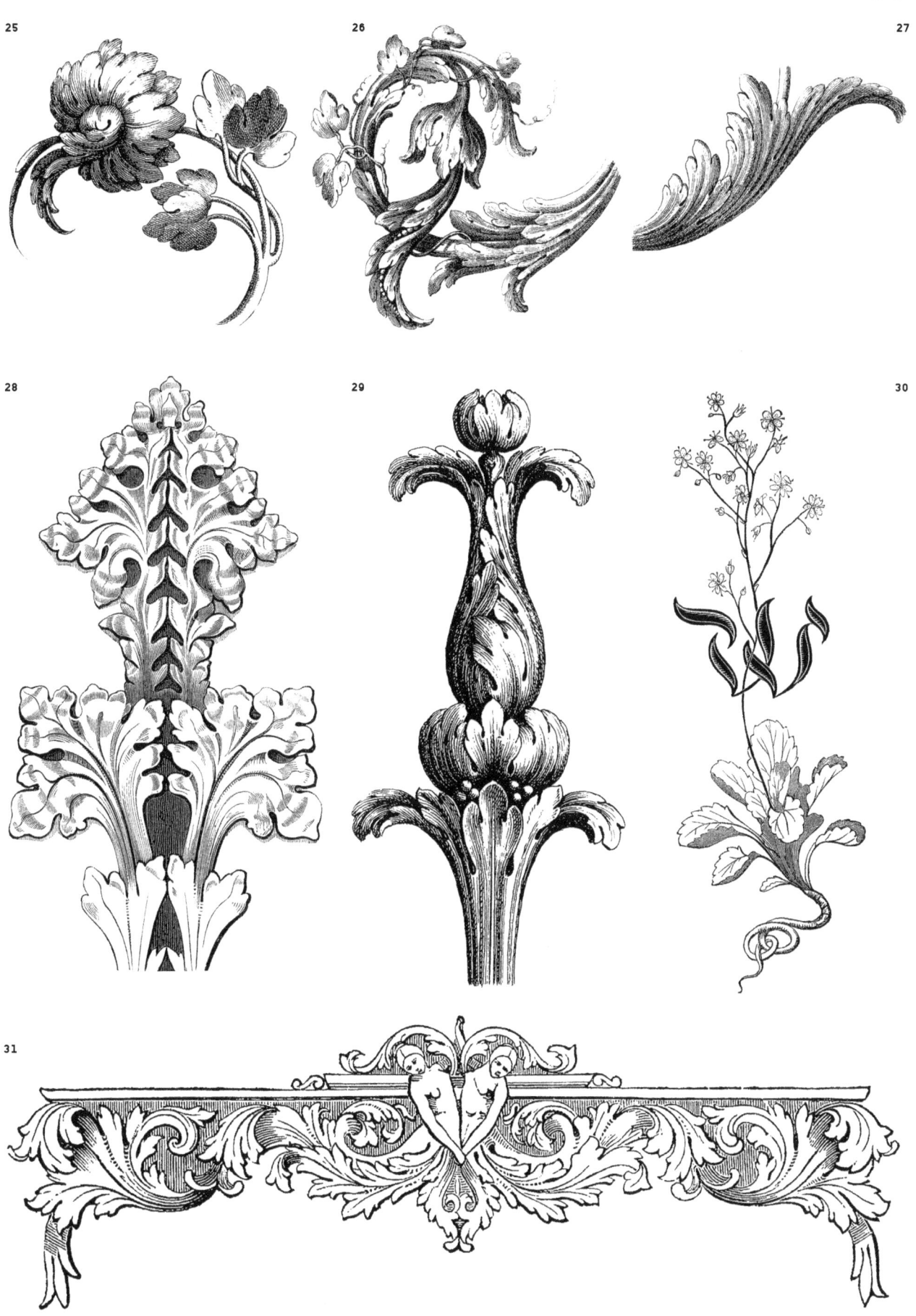

34

35

36

37

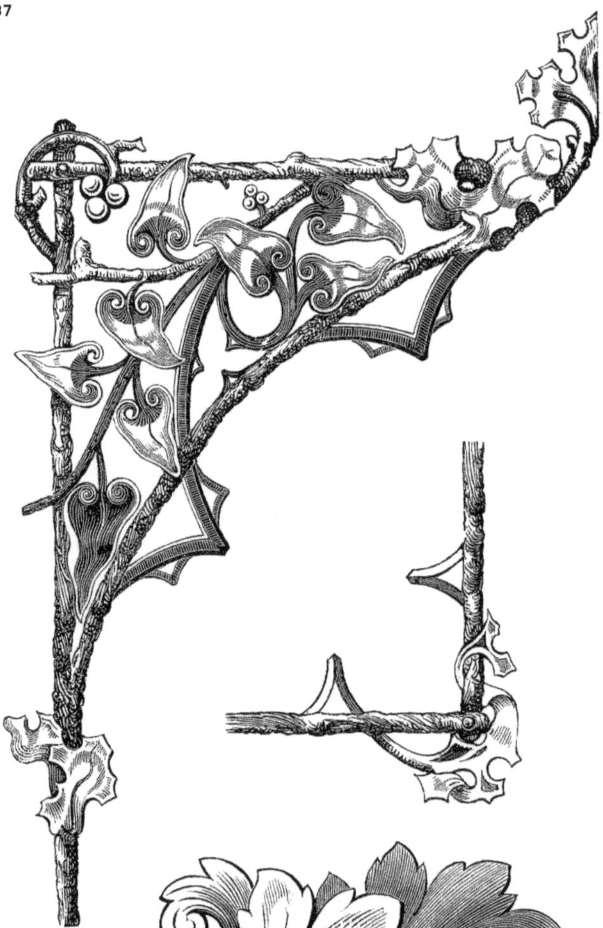

38

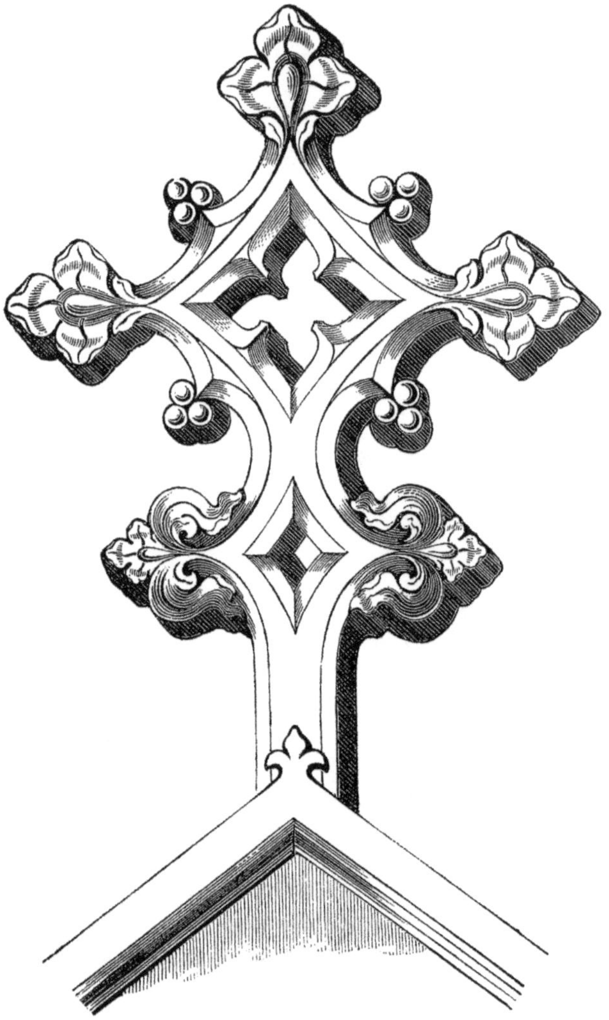

39

40

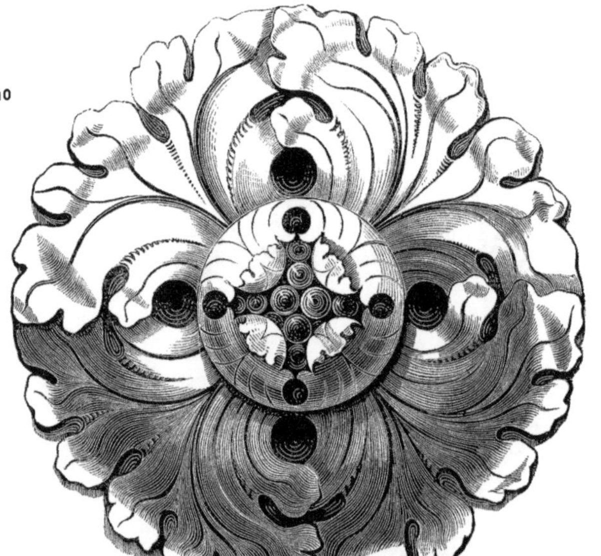

41

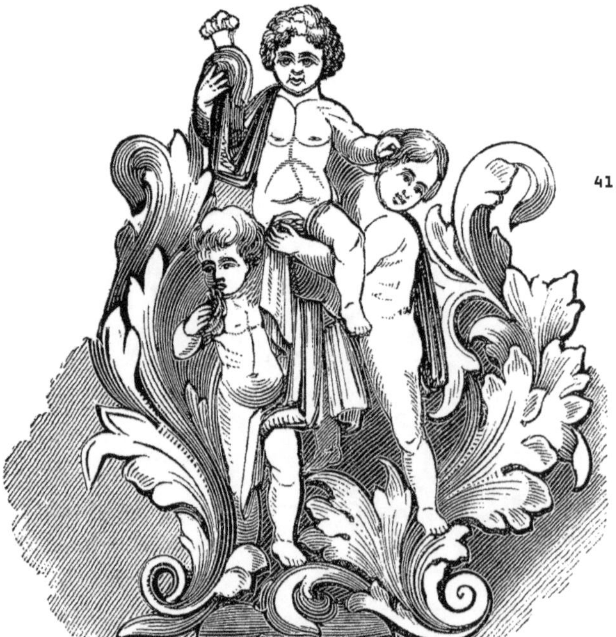

42

43

44

67

68

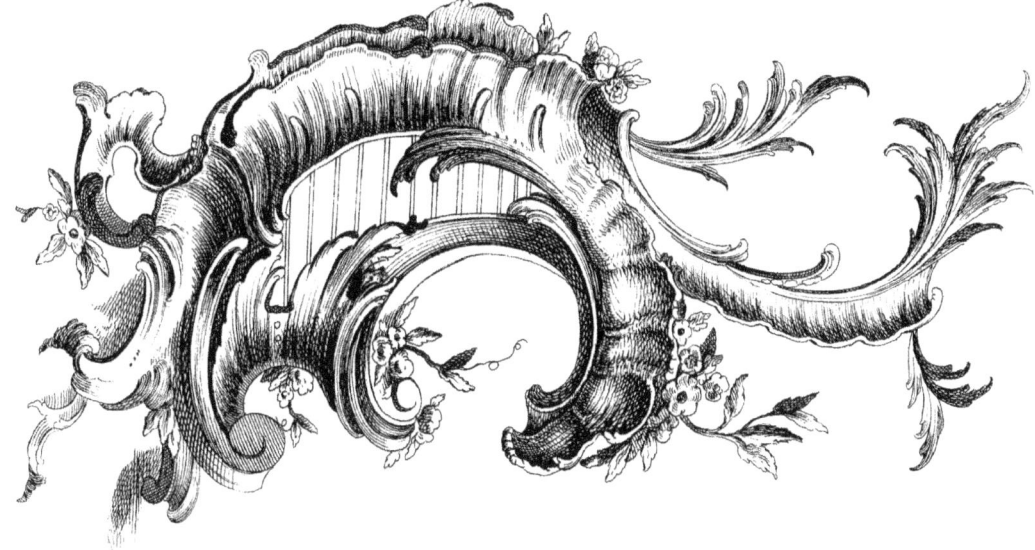

91

92

98

99

100

101

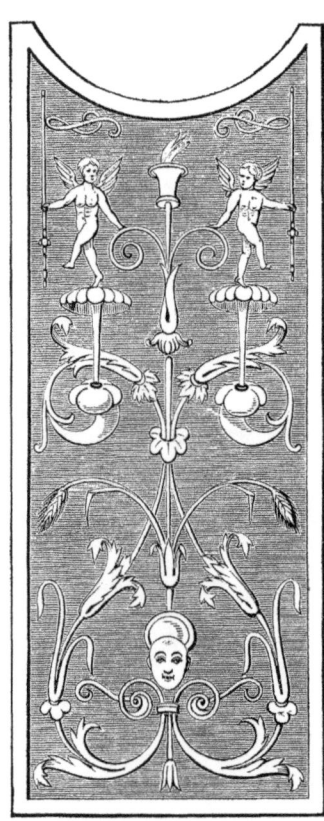

102

103

104

106

105

107

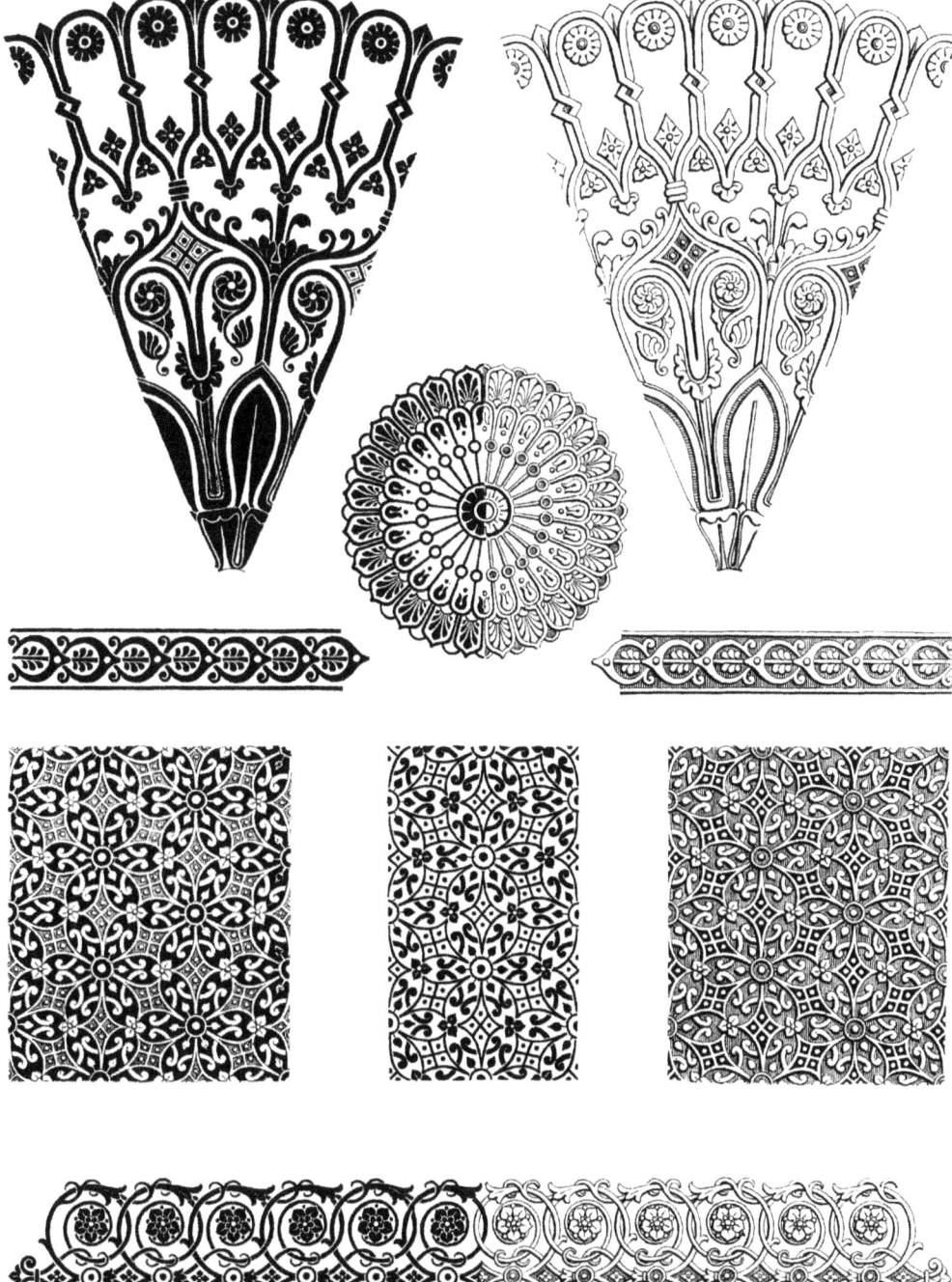

DECEMBER

FEBRUARIUS.

LIST OF ILLUSTRATIONS

A Design for a Curvilinear Foliage
A design for a panel (French)
Design for a Centrepiece
Design for a Centrepiece
Oval motif of tendrils with leaves and whorls of leaves, Johannes Jacobsz Folkema, after Jean Louis Durant, after 1697 - before 1718
Leaf vines with child on carriage, Johann Hinrich Fürst, after Johann Ernst Nicolai, 1685
Two crossed pipes with leaf tendrils coming out, Louis Cossin, after Louis Roupert, 1668
Leaf tendrils, Louis Cossin, after Louis Roupert, 1668
Leaf vine with three flowers and birds, Johannes Jacobsz Folkema, c. 1690 - c. 1700
Two large and two small motifs with leaf tendrils and flowers, Johannes Jacobsz Folkema, c. 1690 - c. 1700
Leaf vine, Paul Androuet Ducerceau, c. 1710
Ornament for gold and silversmiths, Monogrammist AC (engraver), c. 1580 - c. 1700
Design for centrepiece or panel
The Acanthus
Arabesques with acanthus leaves, anonymous, after Johann Leonhard Eisler, 1726 - 1734
Acanthus motif, Cesare Domenichi, after Ludovico Scalzi, 1607
Acanthus motif, Cesare Domenichi, after Ludovico Scalzi, after Pietro Antonio Prisco, 1589 - 1614
Acanthus leaf ornaments
Acanthus leaf ornamental design
Acanthus leaf ornamental design
Architectural ornament
Architectural ornament
Ornamental roundel for a cabinet
Ornament with satan, Bernard Picart, 1720
Floral ornament design
Acanthus vine and tendril
Acanthus leaf ornament
Gothic Finial on Doorway
Acanthus leaf ornament
Ornamental W
Design for a window cornice
Surface decoration with scrolls and grotesques, Heinrich Aldegrever, 1552
Vertical double leaf tendril, René Lochon, after Charles II Errard, 1651
A gothic design for a border and corner
Ornament featuring a Harpy, Bernard Picart, 1715
Ornament with leaf tendrils, Bernard Picart (workshop of), 1683 - 1733
An original design for a corner and end piece
Design for a gable cross
Acanthus leaf ornament
Gothic ornamental roundel design
Ornamental design featuring 3 children
Ornament with cherub, Bernard Picart (workshop of), 1683 - 1733
Ornament with two fasces, Bernard Picart (workshop of), 1683 - 1733
Ornament with shell, Bernard Picart (workshop of), after Bernard Picart, 1683 - 1733
Floral ornament (thorn-apple)
Floral ornament (Water crowfoot)
Floral ornament
Floral ornament
Floral ornament
Floral ornament
Floral ornament
Floral ornament
Floral ornament
Floral ornament
Floral ornament
Volutes of scrollwork, Michel Liénard, c. 1866
Fantasy animals representing the seven deadly sins, Michel Liénard, 1866
Leaf vine with bird-headed winged monster, Michel Liénard, c. 1866
Satyr mask and vines ending in animal heads, Michel Liénard, 1866
Panel with satyr mask between leaf tendrils and scrollwork, Michel Liénard, 1866
Two leaf vine motifs, Michel Liénard, 1866
Two leaf vine motifs, Michel Liénard
Lion and dog on and between leaf vines, Michel Liénard, 1866
Ornaments of branches with leaves, Michel Liénard, 1866
Designs for Three Vertical Ornaments, Gabriel Huquier, Gilles Marie Oppenort, c. 1725 - c. 1750
Ornamental panel design (Elizabethan)
Design for a frieze
Panel with pedestal between two dogs, Alexis Loir (I), c. 1670 - c. 1690
Pilaster End, From the Temple of Apollo
A sketch take from a book cover
Design for a grecian pannel
An Italian design for a panel
Fifteenth-Century Tarsia
Five Ornaments, Master PC, c. 1672 - c. 1676
Rocaille ornaments 2, anonymous, after Franz Xaver Habermann, 1731 - 1775
Rocaille ornaments 3, anonymous, after Franz Xaver Habermann, 1731 - 1775
Rocaille ornaments and window frame, anonymous, after J. Matthaeus Schmahl, 1705 - 1775
Rocaille ornaments and frame, anonymous, after J. Matthaeus Schmahl, 1705 - 1775
Rocaille ornaments with birds, Franz Xaver Habermann (possibly), after Franz Xaver Habermann, 1731 - 1775
Rocaille ornaments with leaf motifs, Franz Xaver Habermann (possibly), after Franz Xaver Habermann, 1731 - 1775
Rocaille ornaments, anonymous, after Franz Xaver Habermann, 1731 - 1775
Rocaille frames, anonymous, after Franz Xaver Habermann, 1731 - 1775
Medallion with Minerva, anonymous, after Aegidius Bichel, 1697
Ornamental leaf with thistle motifs, Daniel Hopfer (I), after anonymous, after c. 1490-before 1536
Bacchus and Ariadne surrounded by leaf-shaped ornaments, Simon Gribelin, 1704
Portrait of William Parsons with leaf ornaments and putti, Simon Gribelin, 1703
Putto with cornucopia and leaf-shaped ornaments, Simon Gribelin, 1704
Time Reveals the Truth, Simon Gribelin, in or before 1704
Three vertical strips with compartments, Daniel Marot (I), 1712
Ornament with two fighting tritons, Ralf Leopold von Retberg, 1846
Ornament with two fantasy creatures and a winged man, Lucas van Leyden, 1528
Ornament with Pan and Syrinx, Gerrit Visscher, 1690 - 1710
Ornament with centaurs and vase, B. Picart
Ornamental cartouche
An Italian design for a border
Ornament with leaf tendril, Gabriel Huquier, after Alexis Peyrotte, 1740
Border sketched from a curious drug bottle
Key-stone sketched from the lower-story window of the imperial assurance office, city
An Arabesque design for a frieze
Italian designed ornaments from Palace Del Te 2
Ornamental letter T
Design for a console, front and side view
Edge with a frieze at the top decorated with leaf tendrils, anonymous, after Paul Birckenhultz, 1571 - 1639

Ornamental shield for title page
Design for a Centrepiece
Ornament with tureen with crown, Bernard Picart (workshop of), 1683 - 1733
Fan-shaped and square ornaments, Gottfried Engelmann, 1798 - 1839
Fan-shaped and square ornaments, Gottfried Engelmann, 1798
Frames and round ornaments, Gottfried Engelmann, 1798 - 1839
Frames and square ornament, Gottfried Engelmann, 1798
Wrought iron gate with floral motifs, anonymous, after Johann Samuel Birckenfeld, 1719 - 1749
Wrought iron gate with floral motifs, anonymous, after Johann Samuel Birckenfeld, 1719
Seed beads with putto and owl, Emanuel Eichel, after Franz Xaver Habermann, 1731 - 1775
Seed beads with putto and wolf, Emanuel Eichel, after Franz Xaver Habermann, 1731 - 1775
Two designs for ironwork with floral motifs, anonymous, after Johann Samuel Birckenfeld, 1694 - 1756
Ironwork with floral motifs, anonymous, after Johann Samuel Birckenfeld, (1694 - 1756)
Ironwork with floral motifs, anonymous, after Johann Samuel Birckenfeld, 1694 - 1756
Ironwork with floral motifs, anonymous, after Johann Samuel Birckenfeld, 1694 -
Decorative vase with fantasy animals, Jakob Gottlieb Thelott, after Christian Friedrich Rudolph, 1718 - 1754
Decorative vase with snail, Jakob Gottlieb Thelott, after Christian Friedrich Rudolph, 1718 - 1760
November, anonymous, after Georg Sigmund Rösch, 1705 - 1766
December, anonymous, after Georg Sigmund Rösch, 1705 - 1766
January, anonymous, after Georg Sigmund Rösch, 1705 - 1766
February, anonymous, after Georg Sigmund Rösch, 1705 - 1766
May, anonymous, after Georg Sigmund Rösch, 1705 - 1766
September, anonymous, after Georg Sigmund Rösch, 1705 - 1766
Title page, Jeremias Falck, after Johann Christian Bierpfaf, c. 1645 - c. 1650
Cartouche with lobe ornament, above and below a mask, Michiel Mosijn, after Gerbrand van den Eeckhout, 1640 - 1655
Commemorative medal in honor of the silver wedding anniversary of Jacob Ploos van Amstel and Sara Rothé, 1746, Pieter Tanjé, 1746
Title page, Thomas Lejuge, after 1697 - before 1718
Three Ornaments with Flowers and a Mask, Paul Androuet Ducerceau, c. 1670 - c. 1690
Three Ornaments with Masks, Paul Androuet Ducerceau, c. 1670 - c. 1690
Ornament of acanthus vines with resting Hercules, Paul Androuet Ducerceau, 1660 - 1690
Ornament of acanthus vines with Hercules with bow and arrow, Paul Androuet Ducerceau, 1660 - 1690
Tetragram and sun and moon in ornamental frame, Bernard Picart (workshop of), after Bernard Picart, 1728
Ornaments with Tetragrammaton and Angels with Circumcision Instruments, Bernard Picart (workshop of), after Bernard Picart, 1683 - 1733
Nicolas Boileau-Despréaux on the Parnassus, Bernard Picart (workshop of), after Bernard Picart, 1728
Nicolas Boileau at his desk with his muse, Bernard Picart (workshop of), after Bernard Picart, 1728
Two puto with conrucopia, Bernard Picart (workshop of), after Bernard Picart, 1728
Venus and Amor in an ornamental frame, Bernard Picart (workshop of), 1724
Memorial to Guillaume de Lamoignon, Bernard Picart, 1718
Meeting between Jacob and Joseph, Bernard Picart (workshop of), after Bernard Picart, 1683 - 1733
Two Panels with Caryatid and Candelabra, Paul Androuet Ducerceau, 1650 - 1703
Two Panels with Candelabra, Paul Androuet Ducerceau, 1650 - 1703
Two panels with candelabra with leaf tendrils, Paul Androuet Ducerceau, 1650 - 1703
Two panels with an Atlantean and Amor with quivers, Paul Androuet Ducerceau, 1650 - 1703
Three floral ornaments, Paul Androuet Ducerceau, 1650 - 1703
Ornaments with acanthus vines and satyrs, Paul Androuet Ducerceau, 1650 - 1703
Candelabra motifs with floral tendrils, Paul Androuet Ducerceau, 1650 - 1703
Acanthus vines, anonymous, after Aegidius Bichel, 1697
Two vertical ornaments of leaf tendrils and with monograms, Gerrit Visscher, 1690
Two vertical ornaments of leaf tendrils and with monograms, Gerrit Visscher, 1690 - 1710
Goldsmith's bouquet in the shape of a circle, Balthazar Moncornet, after Balthasar Le Mersier, 1626
Goldsmith's bouquet in the shape of a pointed oval, Balthazar Moncornet, after Balthasar Le Mersier, 1626
Jewelery bouquet with tendrils, Balthazar Moncornet, after Francois Lefebure, after Jacques Callot, after Nicolas de Son, 1635
Jewelery bouquet with tendrils, Balthazar Moncornet, after Francois Lefebure, after Jacques Callot, after Nicolas de Son, 1635 copy

LEARN MORE

At Vault Editions, our mission is to create the world's most diverse and comprehensive collection of image archives available for artists, designers and curious minds. If you have enjoyed this book, you can find more of our titles available at vaulteditions.com.

REVIEW THIS BOOK

As a small, family-owned independent publisher, reviews help spread the word about our work. We would be incredibly grateful if you could leave an honest review of this title wherever you purchased this book.

JOIN OUR COMMUNITY

Are you a creative and curious individual? If so, you will love our community on Instagram. Every day we share bizarre and beautiful artwork ranging from 17th and 18th-century natural history and scientific illustration, to mythical beasts, ornamental designs, anatomical illustration and more. Join our community of 100K+ people today—search @vault_editions on Instagram.

DOWNLOAD YOUR FILES

STEP ONE

Enter the following web address in your web browser on a desktop computer.

www.vaulteditions.com/pages/tco

STEP TWO

Enter the following unique password to access the download page.

tcoa2384736438sxda

STEP THREE

Follow the prompts to access your high-resolution files.

TECHNICAL ASSISTANCE

For all technical assistance, please email: info@vaulteditions.com

www.ingramcontent.com/pod-product-compliance
Lightning Source LLC
Chambersburg PA
CBHW051332110526
44590CB00032B/4487